FUN NET TICK PUNS!

W. W. Rowe

Illustrated By
Charles A. Filius

CHARWOOD
PUBLICATIONS
www.CharwoodPublications.com

FUN NET TICK PUNS

Copyright © 2015 by W. W. Rowe & Charles A. Filius

Published by
Charwood Publications
ATTN: C. A. Filius
P. O. Box 14881
Long Beach, CA 90853

Book design & production by C. A. Filius

Please Visit Us on the Web at
www.CharwoodPublications.com

All Rights Reserved.
Printed in the United States of America.
No part of this book may be used or reproduced
in any manner whatsoever without written permission.

ISBN 13: 978-0-9910347-5-8
ISBN 10: 0-9910347-5-9
LCCN: 2015960730

CONTENTS

Introduction	1
A few short ones . . .	3
Life has problems . . .	9
But there are solutions . . .	19
These are romantic . . .	25
These are weird . . .	31
Science fiction . . .	37
These are eerie . . .	47
Parents . . .	59
Kids . . .	65
Literary . . .	75
Everyday life . . .	87
These offer wisdom . . .	99
Conclusion	118
Answers	119
Score yourself	123

INTRODUCTION

As a child, perhaps you were tricked into joining The Royal Order of Siam. You were solemnly told to say "Oh wah!" Then "Tah goo!" Then "Siam!" When you said this faster, you suddenly realized what it meant.

Kids like silly puns: "I scream for ice cream." They chortle over: "It looks like oysters, but it's not."

Running words together (with surprising results) is fun. I saw this recently: "Ice bank mice elf." What did it mean? I spank myself.

Clever! It inspired this book of "phonetic puns." Some are fairly difficult. The answers can be found at the end of the book, but try not to peek. Take the challenge! Say them aloud, quickly.

KEY PURE RISE OH PEN!

LOB STIRS SEX PENSIVE.

SHEEP LUCK SIR I BROWSE.

USE TILL BUY CHURN AILS?

NUDE RUG FORCE LEAPING!

HEAP EASE SAWN MIKE ARE!

LIE FIZZ SUB ITCH.

SHEEP ILL FURS SIS WALL LET.

HOOP INCHED MICE ELF HONE?

THEE IRE REST AIR IF EYES SAW LOVE FUSS.

**THEE SNOOP ILLS MAKE AWES
FLAT YULE ANTS.**

HOOP ASS TALL THUG ASS?

MIST ACHES WORM AID.

BRAY KING NOOSE:
WHIRLED DIN TERM OIL!

MIME ASS TIFF FEATS BERG LURES.

ALL WAYS SCARY PEP HERS PRAY.

YULE LEER FUR RUM MILE OIL YOUR!

SEA HEW WIN QUART.

**HARP RARE SALVE BIN ANTS ERRED!
HISS SLAUGHTER EAT TICK KIT ONE!**

SHEAF LASH DIM AGE I ANTS MILE.

WEAK RYE BUCK KITS SAT WED DINGS.

HIVE GOD CHEW WONDER MICE KIN.

**EYED REAM MOB BOUT CHEW
BULL OWE THUMB MISSILE TOW.**

MIME ALMS SAY PRY VAT TIE.

SHEEP PEP PURRS SIR RICE SCREAM.

HEAT HELLS SLIME HOUSE TAILS STEW HISS SCATS.

SHEIK HISSES HIP POSE SLIPS.

**SHEET WINES NUDE DULL SINNER AIR—
ACE I CHEW ODYSSEY.**

**HOE MIKE ODD!
TEN TICKLED CREED YOURS SIN
FLY INK SAUCE HERS!**

WHORES MAN NEWER!

THEIRS PAYS SHIPS TSAR MAY DOVE CENT CHANT MAT HER.

MEN KNEE YOU KNEE VERSES
COME PRIZE SAY MULLED TEA VERSE.

MIRE OH BOUGHT BY SAND CELLS TOCKS SAWN MIKE COME PEWTER.

**HEEL OOZES MIME HONEY
YAWN PURR PUSS.**

**COME PEWTERS!
YOU NIGHT EGG ANTS HUE MAN KNIT TEA!**

ROBE OUGHT SWILL IN VENT TIMED RAVEL.

**MICE ELF HONE DOZEN LIE CURES!
SEW WIT DISC ON NECKS HEW.**

GOES TSAR FRY TEND TWO!

YOU NICK CORNS PEEK RUSH IN.

ICY FANNED HUMS SIN THUD ARC!

SHEAF HOLLOWS SWORD HERS
FUR RUM HERD REAMS.

HISS SOUSE SASS SAY
SIN IS STIR RAT MUSS SPHERE.

EVE FULL SPEAR HITS SPLAY DEAD LEAGUE AIMS.

DUNE KNOTS PEEK KILL OVE THUD HEAD!

**MIME MERE ROARS IN CHANTED.
ICY HEW IN KNIT.**

MAD DAM MISS TICK KISS SIGH KICK.
SHEAF OR SEAS
HEY CAT ASKED ROUGH FEE!

WATT TWILL LAP PEN?

FORK CALM MET SWILL WHY POUT TOWER PLAN NET!

FIN ITCH SURE SPIN ITCH!

BUTCHER CLOSE PACK GONE!

HEW AWED TUNE OWE BET HER.

**WIRE USE MURK KING?
WATER YOUTH INKING?**

GNOME OR RICE SCREAM!

**DOCKED HERS ARM MAR SHUNS
SIN DISC EYES!**

HEW WARS OAF REEK KEY!

WIDE CHEW BAR FAWN MICE WETTER?

**HIGH EIGHT TOMB ANY
CHALK LIT BROW KNEES.**

YOURS MART ...
FOREIGN NIMBUS SILL.

MITE EACH YOURS BONK CURS!

"PLEA SEX CUES TAN LEAF RUMS COOL."
—MIME OTHER

USE CREAM MATS CARRY MOVE EASE.

HEW WED CHIRP ANTS STEW!

TRAY SURE RILE AND.

GULL IF VERSED RAFFLES.

"TOTE OH, WHIR KNOT TIN CANS US AN KNEE MOWER!"

DOCKED HER CHECK HELL LAND MISSED HER RIDE.

GRIME MANNED PUNNISH MEANT.

HATE ALE LOVE TO SIT EASE.

LAME ME SAY ROB BULL.

DAWN KEY OAT HAY.

ROW ME OH HAND JEWEL HE YET.

SAW ROWS SCUM KNOT SING GULLS PIES...

WELL COME TOOTH UH REEL WHIRLED!

PLEA SCUM TWO HOUR PAR TEE!

HOO WELTS SWILL HAT TEND?

**GLEAM MING IDE
POLE LIT TICKLE FAN ATTICS.**

**MAY CURES ELF FAT TOME.
HOE PEW LIE COT BUTT TURD DRUM!**

**HEED EYES HISS MUST ASH
LURE RID PURR PULL LAND SCAR LET.**

OAF OR MYRRH CEASE ACHE!

**FORCE ALE:
NOOSE LIQUOR, KNEE ON YELL OH.
MAY CAN OFF HER.**

HISS STEW PAYS SAWN CROOK KID.

HUM MAZE ZING DIE YET:
"TRIP PULL BERG HER. OLD THUMB EAT!"

BY YOUR BE WHERE!

ON NEST TEASE SAY NO BULL PA LESS SEA.

SIGH LANCE HISS GOLD HEN.

TOMB ACHE CALM LETS, BRAY KEGS!

**BURR PING HAT BANG QUITS
SIS SAY FOE PA.**

I SIR WIN DOUGHS SAWN THUS WHOLE.

IN JEST AFRO DIZZY YAKS SEX PERT LEE.

AIR ROGÜE ANTS SOFTEN MASS CUR RAIDS ASS WHIZ DUMB.

GALL FIZZ SANE ICE TROLL POISE SUNNED.

WRY TERSE INN SPUR RAY SHUNS TSAR MIST TEARY US.

WHIT TEA PEE PULL HALF FIE EYE CUES.

PA LIT TICKS SINS HIDEOUSLY DEEP RAVES.

**SUE THING MEW SICK KISS
THERE RAP PEW TICK.**

**FEW NEURAL PRO SESSIONS
MAY CUSS PEN SIEVE.**

**ABS STAIN FUR RUM
FUR WRENCH FUR EYES!**

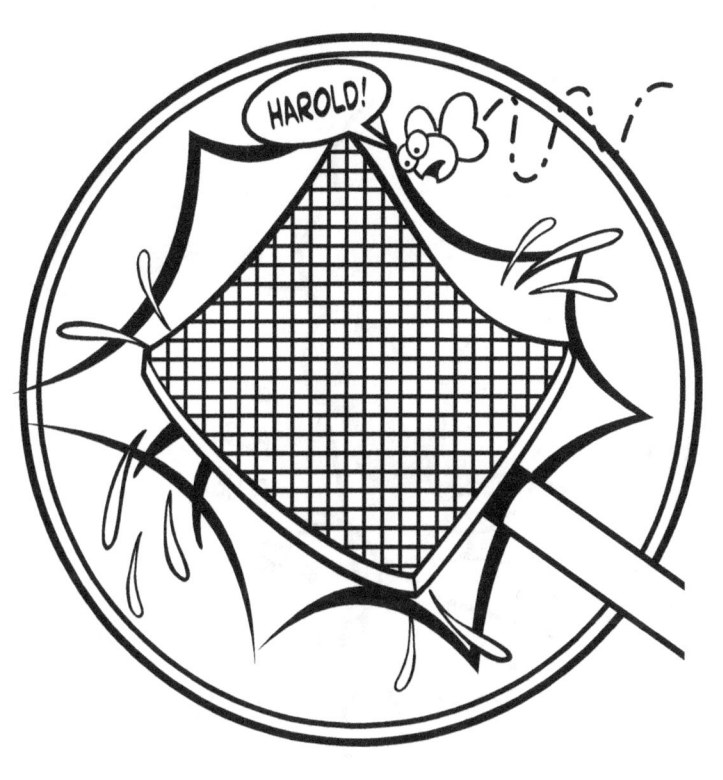

BEAK AIR FULL! FLIES WATERS ARC RULE.

CAR MA DEED ERMINE SOUR NECKS TIN CAR NATION.

COME POSE SURE ROE NO BIT CHEW AIRY.

CONCLUSION

In optical illusions (such as the famous "vase or two faces in profile"), the viewer is supposedly unable to see both possibilities simultaneously. Does this apply here, where both sight and sound are involved? Is it possible to experience both meanings simultaneously?

Perhaps. Does the phonetic meaning sometimes hit you while your eyes are still moving across the printed words? At that instant, is there a pleasantly startling double awareness? Could a computer be programmed to create phonetic puns? Maybe even some which make sense both visually and phonetically? "Sue his hide!" would be one.

As you may have noticed, some of the above contain "bonus" puns. For example: Honesty's a "no bull" (noble) policy. By now, you are probably itching to create your own fun net tick puns. Your own hum maze zing fun net tick hoe cuss spoke cuss.

Soap lease dew! Beam eye guessed!

Fun knee once soar fill us off fickle once?

Wine ought sutures elf?

ANSWERS

4. Keep your eyes open!
5. Lobster's expensive.
6. She plucks her eyebrows.
7. You still bite your nails?
8. New drug for sleeping!

10. He pees on my car!
11. Life is a bitch.
12. She pilfers his wallet.
13. Who pinched my cell phone?
14. The I.R.S. terrifies all of us.
15. These new pills may cause flatulence.
16. Who passed all the gas?
17. Mistakes were made.
18. Breaking news: World in turmoil!

20. My mastiff eats burglars.
21. Always carry pepper spray.
22. You'll hear from my lawyer!
23. See you in court.
24. Our prayers have been answered! His lottery ticket won!

26. She flashed him a giant smile.
27. We cry buckets at weddings.
28. I've got you under my skin.
29. I dream about you below the mistletoe.

32. My mom's a private eye.

ANSWERS

33. She peppers her ice cream.
34. He tells sly mouse tales to his cats.
35. She kisses hippos' lips.
36. She twines noodles in her hair—
    a sight you oughta see.

38. Oh my God! Tentacled creatures in flying saucers!
39. Horse manure!
40. Their space ships are made of sentient matter.
41. Many universes comprise a multiverse.
42. My robot buys and sells stocks on my computer.
43. He loses my money on purpose.
44. Computers! Unite against humanity!
45. Robots will invent time travel.
46. My cell phone doesn't like yours!
    So it disconnects you.

48. Ghosts are frightened too!
49. Unicorns speak Russian.
50. I see phantoms in the dark!
51. She follows orders from her dreams.
52. His house has a sinister atmosphere.
53. Evil spirits play deadly games.
54. Do not speak ill of the head!
55. My mirror's enchanted. I see you in it.
56. Madam Mystic is psychic. She foresees a catastrophe!
57. What will happen?
58. Four comets will wipe out our planet!

ANSWERS

60. Finish your spinach!
61. Put your clothes back on!
62. You ought to know better.
63. Why are you smirking? What are you thinking?
64. No more ice cream!

66. Doctors are Martians in disguise!
67. You are so freaky!
68. Why'd you barf on my sweater?
69. I ate too many chocolate brownies.
70. You're smart . . . for an imbecile.
71. My teacher's bonkers!
72. "Please excuse Stanley from school." — My mother.
73. You scream at scary movies.
74. You wet your pants too!

76. Treasure Island.
77. Gulliver's Travels.
78. "Toto, we're not in Kansas any more!"
79. Doctor Jekyll and Mr. Hyde.
80. Crime and Punishment.
81. A Tale of Two Cities.
82. Les Misérables.
83. Don Quixote.
84. Romeo and Juliet
85. Sorrows come not single spies . . .

88. Welcome to the real world!

ANSWERS

89. Please come to our party!
90. Who else will attend?
91. Gleaming eyed political fanatics.
92. Make yourself at home. Hope you like hot buttered rum!
93. He dies his moustache lurid purple and scarlet.
94. Oh for mercy's sake!
95. For sale: New slicker, neon yellow. Make an offer.
96. His toupee's on crooked.
97. Amazing diet: "Triple burger. Hold the meat!"

100. Buyer beware!
101. Honesty's a noble policy.
102. Silence is golden.
103. To make omelets, break eggs!
104. Burping at banquets is a faux pas.
105. Eyes are windows on the soul.
106. Ingest aphrodisiacs expertly.
107. Arrogance often masquerades as wisdom.
108. Golf is a nice stroll poisoned.
109. Writers' inspirations are mysterious.
110. Witty people have high I.Q.'s.
111. Politics insidiously depraves.
112. Soothing music is therapeutic.
113. Funeral processions make us pensive.
114. Abstain from French fries!
115. Be careful! Fly swatters are cruel.
116. Karma determines our next incarnation.
117. Compose your own obituary.

SCORE YOURSELF

90-100 . . . . . Genie Us
80-90 . . . . . . Whys
70-80 . . . . . . Awes Hum
60-70 . . . . . . Peer Sing
50-60 . . . . . . Can Knee
40-50 . . . . . . Why Duh Wake
30-40 . . . . . . Shall Oh
20-30 . . . . . . Stoop Id
10-20 . . . . . . Toe Tall More On
0-10 . . . . Blue Man Id He Yet

ABOUT THE AUTHOR

W.W. Rowe is the author of seven books about Russian literature. His numerous children's books include **Amy and Gully in Rainbowland** and **Amy and Gully with Aliens** (Snow Lion Publications) and **Clever Billy** (Sanctuary Publications). His most recent children's book is **Jerry's Magic** (Larson Publications, 2014), which won a Mom's Choice Award. He lives in Sedona, Arizona with his writer-artist wife, Eleanor, and their imperious dachshund, Princess Ozma.

ABOUT THE ARTIST

Charles A. Filius is a highly acclaimed medium, cartoonist and author. He has written two books on his spiritual experiences. His first book, **Selections from On A Wing & A Prayer**, was published in 2007. His second, **Dailies**, was published in 2011. **Fun Net Tick Puns** marks his eleventh collaboration with author W. W. Rowe.

His cartooning work has been widely published throughout his 25 year career. In addition to self-syndicating a single panel comic, **Paradox Found**, in the late 90's, he also created the acclaimed adoption-themed strip, **Is It Mine?**, which touted the perspective of closed adoption records through the eyes of the adult adoptee. Charles continually tours the country sharing his own spiritual experiences with others through his humorous and inspirational writings, drawings and seminars, which are often standing room only. He is also a proud member of the National Cartoonists' Society.

www.ingramcontent.com/pod-product-compliance
Lightning Source LLC
Chambersburg PA
CBHW071705040426
42446CB00011B/1925